TAKE TEN YEARS

1910s

Library of Congress Cataloging-in-Publication Data

Sharman, Margaret.
    1910s / written by Margaret Sharman.
        p.   cm. — (Take ten years)
    Includes index.
    Summary: Explores the decade of the 1910s worldwide, a time of great upheaval, including the events surrounding World War I and the Russian Revolution.
    ISBN 0-8114-3074-X
    1. History, Modern—20th century—Juvenile literature.
    [1. History, Modern—20th century.] I. Title. II. Title: Nineteen tens. III. Series.
D425.S53 1992   92–17521
909.82′1—dc20   CIP
                                           AC

Typeset by Multifacit Graphics, Keyport, NJ
Printed in Spain by GRAFO, S.A., Bilbao
Bound in the United States by Lake Book, Melrose Park, IL
1 2 3 4 5 6 7 8 9 0 LB 97 96 95 94 93 92

Acknowledgments

Maps — Jillian Luff of Bitmap Graphics
Design — Neil Sayer
Editor — Caroline Sheldrick

For permission to reproduce copyright material the author and publishers gratefully acknowledge the following:

Cover photographs — Culver Pictures; Sophia Smith Collection; Bettmann Archive; Brown Brothers; The Hulton Picture Co.

page 4 — (from top) Popperfoto, e.t. archive, Popperfoto, Topham; page 5 — (from top) Topham, Topham, e.t. archive, Topham, Topham; page 8 — The Bettmann Archive; page 9 — (top) The Bettmann Archive, (bottom) e.t. archive; page 10 — The Vintage Magazine Co; page 11 — Brown Brothers; page 12 — The Bettmann Archive; page 13 — Topham; page 14 — (top) The Hulton Picture Company, (bottom) Mary Evans Picture Library; page 15 — Brown Brothers; page 16 (top) The Hulton Picture Company, (bottom) e.t. archive; page 17 — (top) Topham, (bottom) All-Sport Photographic Ltd; page 18 — Brown Brothers; page 19 — (left) Brown Brothers, (right) Popperfoto; page 20 — (left) ©ADAGP, Paris and DACS, London 1991/Bridgeman Art Library, London, (bottom) e.t. archive; page 21 — The Hulton Picture Company; page 22 — Topham; page 23 — e.t. archive; page 25 — e.t. archive; page 26 — (left) The Hulton Picture Company, (right) Popperfoto; page 27 — Popperfoto; page 29 — (right) Popperfoto, (left) e.t. archive; page 30 — (top left) Topham, (bottom left) e.t. archive; page 31 — Topham; page 32 — e.t. archive; page 33 — (left) Popperfoto, (right) Topham; page 34 — The Vintage Magazine Co; page 35 — (left) The Bettmann Archive, (right) Topham; page 36 — (left and bottom right) e.t. archive, (top right) The Hulton Picture Company; page 37 — (top) Popperfoto, (bottom) ECOSCENE; page 38 — Brown Brothers; page 39 — Popperfoto; page 40 — (left) e.t. archive, (right) The Vintage Magazine Co; page 41 — (center) Brown Brothers, (right) Topham; page 42 — (left) Popperfoto, (right) Brown Brothers; page 43 — (top) The Hulton Picture Company, (center) Topham, (bottom) e.t. archive; page 44 — (from top) The Vintage Magazine Company, Martin Breese/Retrograph Archive, The Advertising Archives; page 45 — The Advertising Archives

TAKE TEN YEARS

1910s

MARGARET SHARMAN

RSVP
RAINTREE
STECK-VAUGHN
P U B L I S H E R S
The Steck-Vaughn Company

Austin, Texas

Contents

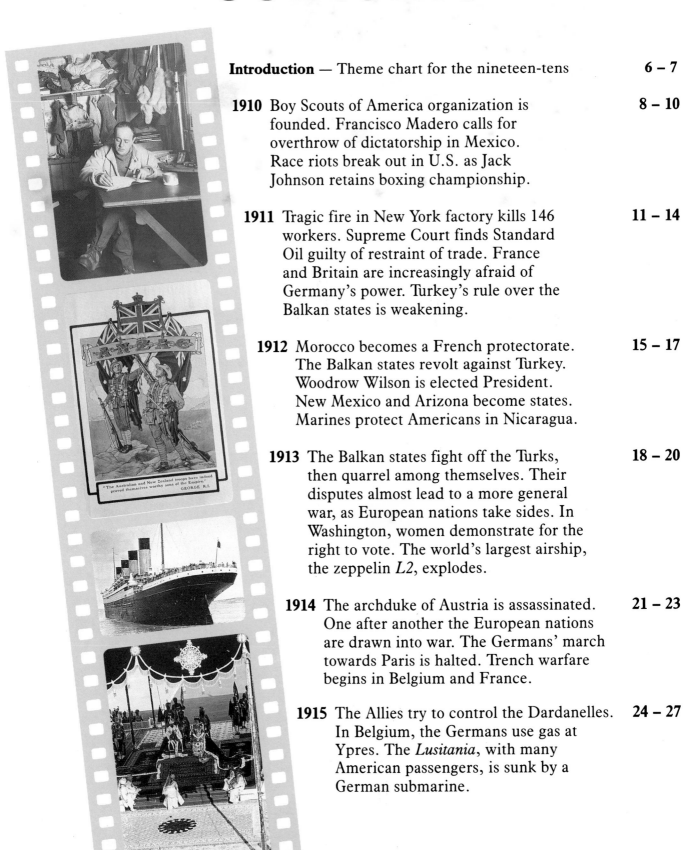

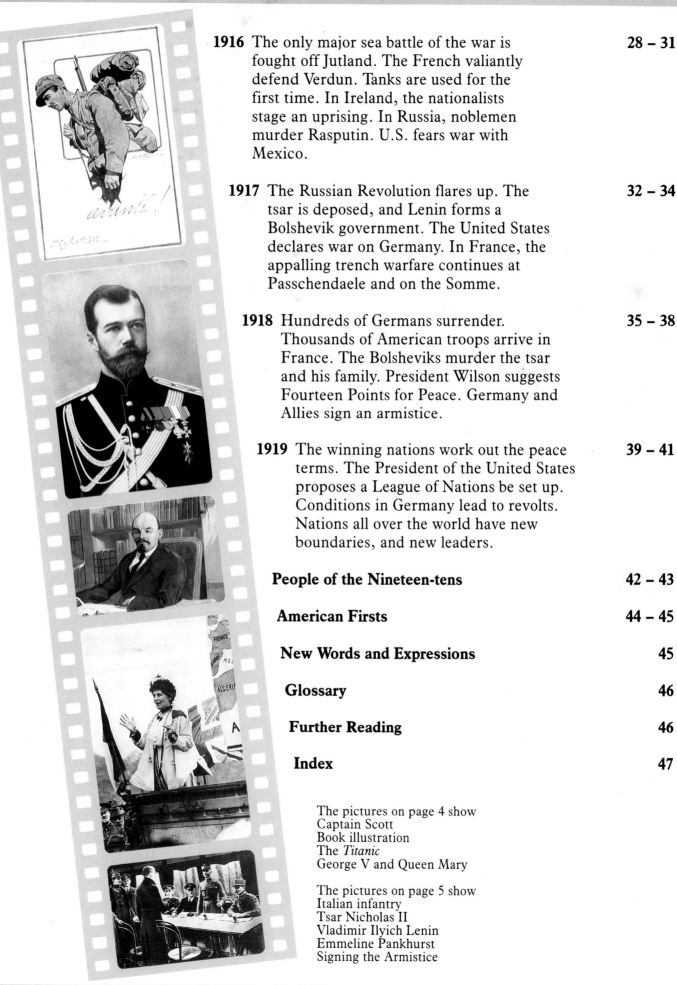

The pictures on page 4 show
Captain Scott
Book illustration
The *Titanic*
George V and Queen Mary

The pictures on page 5 show
Italian infantry
Tsar Nicholas II
Vladimir Ilyich Lenin
Emmeline Pankhurst
Signing the Armistice

Introduction

The 1910s saw the end of an old way of life in Europe. World War I, known as the Great War, is the dividing line. Before the war, wealthy landowners all over Europe formed an upper class which was able to keep up a high standard of living. Their houses were run by servants, from the butler and housekeeper to the kitchenmaid. The sons of these wealthy families went to private schools (called public schools in England). Here they were taught a strict code of honor. They were to be their countries' leaders. They believed it was right to die for one's family and one's country.

These young men became the officers on both sides in the war. They led their men "over the top" of the trenches, and were often the first to die. The men they led had joined up with great enthusiasm. They too believed in their country, right or wrong. On both sides, they suffered appalling hardships. Millions died in the mud of France and Belgium, and on the Russian front. Their graves are still honored today. Those who survived no longer believed that war was "glorious." They went home believing that now things would be different.

Women in England and the United States had been protesting for some years against the lower status of women. Many joined the suffragettes, and fought for the right to vote. During the war they were able to do useful work outside their homes. Their self-respect and self-reliance grew as they nursed the wounded, and did the jobs of men away fighting in France.

In America, nobody wanted to go to war. But when the Germans sank our ships we joined the Allies. America came out of the war with our lands intact and our economy in good shape. In Europe, and in the East, the survivors faced poverty and even starvation. Their towns were in ruins. The fight for the rights of ordinary men and women was beginning. In Germany, Italy, and Russia, leaders who promised a better world were sure of a great many supporters.

YEARS	WORLD AFFAIRS
1910	Revolution in Mexico
1911	Germans land in Morocco. Italians land in Tripoli, Libya.
1912	Home Rule for Ireland debated. Morocco becomes French protectorate. Italians occupy Libya.
1913	Suffragettes call for the vote.
1914	World War I begins, because of Balkan crisis.
1915	World War I Serbia defeated.
1916	World War I U-boats sink neutral ships.
1917	World War I Russian Revolution
1918	World War I ends.
1919	Versailles Peace Treaty signed. Poland becomes independent.

WARS & CIVIL DISORDER	PEOPLE	EVENTS
King of Portugal ousted.	Edison invents kinetophone. President Taft opens baseball season. Jack Johnson keeps boxing title. Violinist Kreisler plays in London.	Boy Scouts of America is formed. South Africa becomes part of British Commonwealth. Halley's Comet is close to Earth.
	King George V crowned in England. Emperor Pu Yi is deposed in China. Marie Curie wins Nobel Prize.	Triangle shirtwaist factory fire Amendment proposed to elect senators by popular vote.
First Balkan War U. S. Marines in Nicaragua	Wilson becomes President. Native American Jim Thorpe is big winner in Olympics.	Native Congress formed in Africa. *Titanic* disaster Two new states in U.S.
Turkish government overthrown. Unrest in Balkans	Wilson personally delivers State of Union message to Congress. Isadora Duncan's children drowned.	Suffragettes march in D.C. Americans pay income tax.
Battles at Mons, Ypres, Tannenburg, Falklands	Von Hindenburg leads German armies. Pearl White is movie favorite.	Clayton Antitrust Act passed. Volcano erupts in Japan.
Dardanelles campaign	Mustafa Kemal leads Turks at Dardanelles. Anzacs win honor. Nurse Edith Cavell is shot. Rupert Brooke, poet, dies.	Gas used in war for first time. *Lusitania* is sunk. Telephone message sent across Atlantic.
Battles of Jutland, Verdun, the Somme Irish Nationalists proclaim republic.	Jeannette Rankin is first woman elected to Congress. Wilson reelected President. Lloyd George becomes British prime minister.	Tanks used for first time. Russian nobles kill Rasputin.
Battles of Passchendaele, Caporetto	Lenin takes over in Moscow. Balfour pledges help to the Jews. Buffalo Bill dies.	Hindenburg Line built. America enters the war.
Battle of the Marne	The "Red Baron" is shot down. Wilfred Owen, poet, killed. Lawrence of Arabia leads Arabs against Turks.	Armistice signed. Russian Tsar executed. Influenza epidemic Million women in U.S. factories
Unrest in Germany Students demonstrate in Peking.	President Wilson asks for a League of Nations. Dempsey becomes boxing champion. Mussolini founds Fascist party.	American women get vote. German fleet sunk at Scapa Flow. Prohibition Amendment is ratified.

1910

REVOLUTION IN MEXICO

November, Mexico City Popular liberal landowner, Francisco Madero, has called for a nationwide revolution to overthrow the dictatorship of General Porfirio Díaz. While Mexico's economy has been improving under Díaz, most of the benefits have gone to the already rich. Most Mexicans continue to exist in the worst kind of poverty. The common people are ready to rise up against their oppressors in the hope of obtaining a better life.

BOY SCOUTS OF AMERICA FORMED

Feb. 8, Washington Incorporation papers for the Boy Scouts of America were filed here today by William D. Boyce. While on business in London last year, Mr. Boyce learned about the British Scout movement when a boy helped him find his way through a thick fog and would not accept a tip. The youngster said he was a Scout and not permitted to receive payment for doing a good deed. Much impressed, Boyce and other leaders are recruiting American boys who want to learn "patriotism, courage, self-reliance and kindred virtues."

In 1907, London-born Lord Baden-Powell founded the original Boy Scout organization. From his observations while serving in the British Army, he decided that English boys did not get enough experience in outdoor life or physical training. This led him to start the Boy Scout organization, which has now spread to our own nation.

X-RAY MACHINE HELPS DOCTORS REMOVE NAIL FROM BOY'S LUNG

Feb. 27, New York When Jacob Miller's father brought his nine-year-old son to Beth Israel Hospital, worried about the child's mysterious weight loss, doctors were at first baffled. Then Dr. Francis Huber, head of the children's ward, took an X ray that clearly showed a one-inch-long nail in one of Jacob's lungs. Jacob had not told his father about swallowing the nail because he was afraid of being punished. Surgeons used X-ray pictures to guide them in removing the nail. They made an incision in the boy's neck and were able to remove the nail with forceps.

Since Wilhelm Roentgen discovered X rays in 1895, many doctors have been using this new technology to examine broken bones.

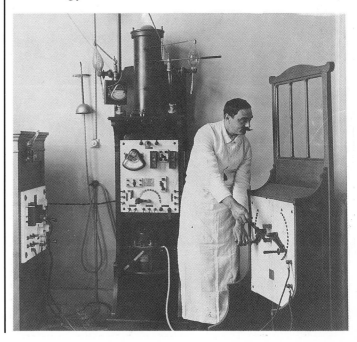

EDISON INVENTS TALKING PICTURES

Aug. 27, West Orange, N.J. Thomas Edison today showed a small but fascinated group his new "kinetophone." This is a machine that combines the sound of a phonograph with the pictures of a movie camera. With this device, both sound and image can be recorded at the same time. Edison has been developing this for the last two years.

THE HUNTING PRESIDENT IS HOME

June 19, New York Mr. Theodore ("Teddy") Roosevelt was given a big welcome here today. The ex-President has spent ten months hunting in British East Africa. His party shot over 10,000 animals. The African hunters call him Bwana Tumbo: Mr. Big Stomach! Teddy bears are also stout; they are named after Teddy Roosevelt.

President Roosevelt enjoys picnicking with his family.

JOHNSON DEFENDS TITLE

July 4, Reno, Nevada Jack Johnson successfully defended his world heavyweight boxing title, knocking out Jim Jeffries in the 15th round. Johnson has held the title since 1908 when he became the first Negro to become champion. Unfortunately, race riots broke out in many parts of the country immediately after Johnson won. Many people have found it hard to accept the idea of a Negro boxing champion.

SOUTH AFRICA BECOMES A DOMINION

July 1, Pretoria The Union of South Africa became a dominion today, becoming part of the British Commonwealth. The official languages are English and Afrikaans, a kind of Dutch. The government consists of British-born and Afrikaaner members of parliament, who are all Europeans. Africans are not allowed to run for parliament.

PORTUGAL LOSES ITS KING

Oct. 5, Lisbon Portugal was once a leading European nation. In the last hundred years it has been very unstable. Today there has been a coup against King Manoel. After bloody fighting in the capital he fled to Gibraltar. The army and navy, which led the coup, have proclaimed the country of Portugal a republic.

A NEW DANCE CRAZE

July 1, New York The latest dance craze, the tango, can now be seen in fashionable ballrooms around town. Long, slow steps alternate with short, quick ones. No one is quite sure of the origins of this Latin American step, but it is very popular in Buenos Aires, Argentina, and even in Paris. It is a romantic dance and many clergymen are concerned about its provocative appeal and are speaking out against it from their pulpits.

NEWS IN BRIEF . . .

TAFT PLAYS BALL

April 10, Washington President Taft threw out the first ball of the new baseball season at the American League's opening game between the Washington Nationals and the Philadelphia Athletics. Taft, who enjoys sports, is the first President to perform this symbolic act.

A FASHION SENSATION

Sept., Paris Women of fashion no longer walk — they hobble! The new skirts are so tight at the ankle that walking is almost impossible. The pope is shocked by the new fashion and has publicly condemned it. Most ladies wear the skirts with a hidden slit or pleat, so that it is easier to move.

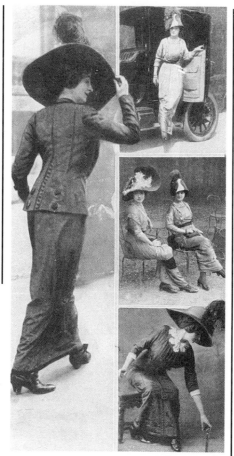

Reduced to a delicate toddle in hobble skirts

VIOLINIST PLAYS A NEW CONCERTO

Nov. 10, London Austrian violinist Fritz Kreisler today played Mr. Edward Elgar's new violin concerto with the Philharmonic Orchestra. The composer was conducting. Mr. Kreisler has played the violin since he was seven. He is one of the world's most brilliant musicians.

WATCH OUT FOR HALLEY'S COMET

May 21, California Scientists believe that the earth is now actually traveling through the tail of Halley's Comet. The Comet is now the closest to the earth it will ever reach. In spite of scientists' reassurances, some people think its tail lets out poisonous gases. They are buying ''comet pills'' and boarding up their houses in case of a disaster. Halley's Comet will return in 75 years.

1911

FIRE KILLS 146

March 24, New York Fire engulfed the Triangle shirtwaist factory here today, killing 146 workers. Most of the victims were young girls. The fire started on payday, shortly before the workers were due to leave for home. The raging flames spread quickly, before any possible escape. Some workers were fatally burned, while others fell to their death when they jumped from upper-floor windows.

While the building had only one fire escape, city inspectors had classified it as fireproof. This tragedy raises questions about the quality of our city fire inspections.

AMERICAN WOMAN BECOMES PILOT

Aug. 1, New York The Aero Club of America has granted a pilot's license to Miss Harriet Quimby. This makes Miss Quimby the first woman pilot licensed in the United States. Madame Dutrie of France was the first woman in the world to hold a pilot's license. Miss Quimby is the second.

She learned to fly at the Moisant Aviation School on Long Island. When taking the test for her license, Miss Quimby came close to equaling a world record. She skillfully managed to land her plane within 7 feet, 9 inches of a target area. The record is 5 feet, 4 inches.

Charred ruins left by Triangle factory fire.

COURT HOLDS OIL TRUST ILLEGAL

May 15, Washington The U.S. Supreme Court found today that the Standard Oil Company is guilty of restraint of trade and that the company must be dissolved. The court also held, however, that the Sherman Antitrust Law does not forbid all trade monopolies but only those that are judged "unreasonable" in restraining trade. Senator Robert M. La Follette of Wisconsin immediately condemned this interpretation.

FIRST INDIANAPOLIS 500-RUN

May 30, Indianapolis The Indianapolis Motor Speedway, which opened in 1909, was the scene today of its first 500-mile race. National driving champion, Ray Harroun, won by tearing around the track at a thrilling 74.59 miles per hour in his locally built Marmon.

ENGLISH ROYAL EVENTS
A KING IS CROWNED

June 22, London Today King George V and Queen Mary were crowned in Westminster Abbey. The Abbey was completely full. The congregation included lords, archbishops, members of Parliament, and representatives of the British Empire. The ceremony followed very ancient coronation customs. Movie cameras filmed the scene outside the Abbey. They were not allowed to go inside.

All but two of England's rulers were crowned in this great church. Westminster Abbey was built in the 1200s in the French Gothic style.

Next month the king's eldest son, David, will travel to Caernarfon Castle, where the Welsh people will welcome him as their new prince of Wales. He is next in line to the throne.

CELEBRATIONS IN INDIA

Dec. 12, Delhi King George of England has been crowned emperor of India in front of a huge crowd. The princes of India were all there, in their splendid silk robes and jewelled turbans. The king announced that in the future Delhi, and not Calcutta, would be the capital of India.

King George V and Queen Mary in India.

GERMANS LAND IN MOROCCO

July 2, Agadir The Germans have sent a gunboat to Agadir, in Morocco. The French are alarmed. Morocco has been under French protection since 1906. Germany has a large army and has become very powerful. The French and British fear that Germany may be a threat to world peace. They will hold talks with the Germans as soon as possible. Meanwhile the Austrians and the British are building up their navies.

LAST EMPEROR IS DEPOSED

Dec. 29, Peking The Chinese people have ended the Manchu dynasty which ruled China for 260 years. The five-year-old emperor, Pu Yi, has left his palace. Dr. Sun Yat-Sen, the revolutionary leader, has become the first president of the republic. He plans to modernize China. For a start, he has forbidden men to wear pigtails. This hairstyle was introduced in the 17th century by the first emperor of the Manchu dynasty.

DIRECT VOTE FOR SENATORS

June 12, Washington The Senate voted to amend the Constitution in order to change the system by which they are elected. Senators are now chosen by their state legislatures. The proposed amendment would allow them to be elected by direct popular vote for six-year terms.

ROYALISTS DEFEATED IN PORTUGAL

Oct. 3, Lisbon There are still many people who want King Manoel back. Their makeshift army was finally defeated today by the republicans. The new government says all lords and dukes must now be called plain "Mister." Monks and nuns have been forced to leave Portugal, as the republicans are against the Church.

ITALY CAPTURES NORTH AFRICAN PORT

Nov. 1, Tripoli, Libya Italian marines have landed at Tripoli in Libya, which is under Turkish rule. The Turks are neglecting their once-powerful empire. Italy has bombed towns and shelled ports. Countries in the Balkans are unhappy to be ruled by Turkey. They may seize the chance to rebel while Turkey and its empire is weak.

All pigtails must go, by order of the republic.

NEWS IN BRIEF . . .

CARS ARE EASIER TO START

Nov. 1, Detroit Louis Chevrolet, a Swiss-born car maker, is going to sell cheap cars. They will compete with Ford's Model T, and with General Motors' Cadillac. This car is being fitted with a self-starter. Owners will be able to turn the engine on by the flick of a switch. The present starting handles sometimes kick like a mule. Doctors say they will be glad to see the end of an injury called "starter's arm"!

PROGRESSIVES SEEK REFORM

Jan. 21, Washington Senator Robert La Follette of Wisconsin will lead the new National Progressive Republican League, which seeks to reform and liberalize the Republican party. The group wants to nominate a progressive at the next party convention in 1912. These reformers also support sterner laws against corrupt business practices.

RAGTIME IS A WINNER

June 26, New York A million copies of "Alexander's Ragtime Band" have been sold in America. Irving Berlin's tune is the greatest hit of all time. It is just right for the turkey trot. Critics say this dance is "disgusting" and "indecent." One young lady has even been jailed for dancing it. But with music like this, who can resist the temptation? Another new Berlin hit is "Everybody's Doin' It." It was sung by the chorus of the *Ziegfeld Follies'* review in New York.

FRENCHWOMAN WINS AWARD

Dec. 10, Paris Mme. Marie Curie has been awarded her second Nobel Prize. In spite of this great achievement, she cannot join the French Academy of Science, because she is a woman. Mme. Curie has extracted pure radium from a rock called pitchblende. You need about six tons of the rock to produce only one tiny gram of radium!

WHAT THE FASHIONABLE SET IS WEARING THIS SEASON

Autumn, New York Women's fashions are freer and more natural than they have ever been before. Women no longer have to be elaborately corseted to achieve the unnaturally curved S-shaped style. The move has generally been away from flounces and frills. Skirts are long and straight. Blouses have a V-shaped neckline. Most ladies have coats with fur collars, and carry fur muffs to match. Ladies driving the new motorcars wear veils over their faces, and goggles over their eyes.

While gentlemen may be formally dressed on occasion, in the country they often wear tweed jackets and plus fours—trousers that reach the knee—and stockings.

1912

HOME RULE FOR IRELAND
ULSTER AGAINST HOME RULE

May 2, London The British government wants Ireland to rule itself. It has introduced a Home Rule Bill. If this bill is passed, Ireland will have its own parliament. Protestants living in Ulster — the Ulster Unionists — do not want home rule. They are afraid that an Irish government would consist of Catholics only. Most Ulster people are descendants of Scottish and English immigrants. They want to stay within the United Kingdom.

LAWRENCE WORKERS STRIKE

Jan. 12, Lawrence, Mass. Workers in the woolen and cotton mills here are striking to protest a pay cut. They get 16 cents per hour. When the state legislature reduced the work week from 56 to 54 hours for women and children, who make up most of the work force, paychecks were cut. The workers want a 15 percent raise for the 54-hour week. They are backed by a powerful union, the Industrial Workers of the World.

NEW FRENCH PROTECTORATE PROCLAIMED

July 1, Morocco By a treaty signed in Fez, Morocco will in future be a French protectorate. The Germans have been asked to leave. In exchange, they will get 600,000 square miles of French territory in the Congo. No Moroccan or Congolese was invited to the talks that led to the treaty.

FIGHTING FOR THEIR RIGHTS

Jan. 8, Pretoria, South Africa Africans and liberal whites in the Union of South Africa have formed the South African Native National Congress. This country was created by the British in 1910 from several of their southern Africa colonies: Natal, Orange Free State, Cape Colony, and Transvaal. Now some of its people are concerned about new laws that restrict African education, wages, and land rights. This new Congress hopes the government will listen to the African point of view.

Massachusetts militiamen keep strikers from entering the mill. The workers want their 16-cents-per-hour wages increased 15 percent.

WOMEN WANT VOTING EQUALITY

March 1, London This afternoon a group of women walked along three of London's smartest streets. Their hands were hidden in fur muffs. Then out of the muffs they pulled hammers and iron bars. The women smashed almost all the shop windows. They are suffragettes, who demand that women should be allowed to vote. Their leader, Mrs. Emmeline Pankhurst, drove to Downing Street and smashed the windows of No. 10, where the prime minister lives. She will go to prison.

Mrs. Pankhurst being arrested. Earlier suffragettes did not take part in acts of violence.

WAR FLARES IN BALKANS

Nov. 30, Sofia, Bulgaria Bulgaria, Romania, Serbia, Montenegro, and Greece have formed the "Balkan League." The League is fighting Turkey and its dwindling empire. It has pushed the Turks out of provinces given them by treaty in the 19th century. The Turks governed these provinces very badly. For the first time aeroplanes are watching the movement of enemy troops.

DEMOCRAT ELECTED TO WHITE HOUSE

Nov. 5, Washington The Democrats have won the presidential election. Woodrow Wilson succeeds William Taft as President of the United States. He said the country needs "New Freedom" in politics, and a strong government. He is also concerned about individual rights and freedom.

HUNDREDS DROWN IN DISASTER

April 15, New York Towards midnight the liner *Titanic*, on her first voyage, hit an iceberg, which stripped the metal side from one end to the other. The passengers found there was not enough room on the lifeboats for them all. Over 1,580 people drowned. The radio operator, who survived, wrote:

"Smoke and sparks were rushing out of her funnel. There must have been an explosion, but we heard none. We only saw the big stream of sparks. The ship was turning gradually on her nose — like a duck that goes for a dive. I had only one thing in mind — to get away from the suction. The band was still playing. I guess all of them went down . . . I swam with all my might. I suppose I was 150 feet away when the *Titanic* . . . began to settle — slowly."

AMERICAN INDIAN HERO OF OLYMPICS

July 22, Stockholm A record number of competitors took part in the Olympic Games. The hero of the games is an American Indian named Jim Thorpe. He won both the pentathlon (5 events) and the decathlon (10 events). Although Thorpe claims he does no special training, he is undoubtedly the best all-round athlete in history.

For the first time, the games were accompanied by broadcast commentaries.

The opening ceremony of the Olympic Games.

Jim Thorpe, champion American runner.

THE ITALIANS ARE STAYING IN LIBYA

Oct. 18, Tripoli By a treaty signed today, Italy's occupation of Libya is legal. The Turks have given in. They are sending their troops to their Balkan provinces. Trouble is brewing for them there, too.

CHURCHILL MODERNIZES BRITISH NAVY

July 22, London Mr. Winston Churchill became first lord of the British Admiralty last October. He has asked the government for money to improve the fleet. He wants all warships' engines to run on oil, rather than coal. Mr. Churchill is alarmed at the strength of Germany's navy.

NEWS IN BRIEF . . .

TWO NEW STATES JOIN UNION

Feb. 14, Washington Last month New Mexico was taken over by the United States as its 47th state. Today one of the states next to it, Arizona, has become the 48th state. Both states are in the Southwest. Two more stars, representing the new states, will be added to the American flag. There are 13 stripes on the American flag. They are a reminder that our country originally had 13 states.

ICE IS NO SUBSTITUTE FOR WATER

Jan. 9, New York Shoppers watched in horror as a skyscraper burned to the ground. Fire fighters had no water. It was so cold that fire engines were covered with ice. Pipes all over the city have frozen and most houses are without any water at all.

NEW RUSSIAN NEWSPAPER

May 5, Moscow A new newspaper, *Pravda*, is on sale in Russia. It is the official paper of the Bolshevik party, and is run by Joseph Stalin. "Pravda" means "truth" in Russian.

MARINES LAND IN NICARAGUA

Aug. 4, Washington About 100 U.S. Marines have just landed in Nicaragua to protect American citizens and property in that country. American banks have had increasing control over Nicaragua's finances since 1911. Rebel forces are opposed to the American presence in their country. They have seized vessels belonging to a large American syndicate that now operates steamship and rail lines in Nicaragua. President Porfirio Díaz asked that Americans use their own forces to protect their many interests in his country.

1913

TROUBLE IN THE BALKANS

YOUNG TURKS DISMISS TREATY

Jan. 23, Constantinople The government has been overthrown by a political party called the Young Turks. They object to a treaty signed last month with the Balkan League. It stated that Turkey should give up its lands in Europe. The Young Turks want Turkey to keep Adrianople. To win it back, Turkey has attacked Bulgaria.

BALKANS STAGE A FREE-FOR-ALL

July 31, Bulgaria In May it was agreed that lands that were once Turkish should be divided among the members of the Balkan League. But they are quarreling about how to divide them. First Bulgaria attacked the Serbs. While they were fighting, the Turks seized Adrianople. The Romanians have now invaded part of Bulgaria.

BALKANS HAVE NEW BOUNDARIES

Aug. 10, Bucharest, Romania By a peace treaty signed today, the Balkan countries have agreed on how to divide the freed lands. Each country except Bulgaria has gained much territory. A new country, Albania, has been created. The Balkan quarrels almost led to a European war. Austria and Russia were ready to take opposite sides in the argument. The British foreign secretary has said, "We are sitting on gunpowder."

SUFFRAGETTES PARADE

March 3, Washington Holding banners that read "Votes for Women" and "Tell Your Troubles to Woodrow," suffragettes paraded here today. On this day before Woodrow Wilson's inauguration, crowds lined the streets both cheering and jeering the marchers. For a long time women's demand for the right to vote had been treated as something of a joke. However, several states already allow women to vote, and more and more women are joining the fight for suffrage. Our new President may soon find votes for women becoming a very serious national issue.

A Missouri suffragette band in Washington, D.C.

AMERICANS ARE TO PAY TAXES

Feb. 3, Washington For the first time since the Civil War, Americans will have to pay an income tax. Congress has to amend the Constitution to make this legal. This will be the 16th Amendment to the Constitution.

WILSON ADDRESSES CONGRESS ON THE STATE OF THE UNION

April 8, Washington   For the first time in 112 years, a President appeared in person before a joint session of the Congress to deliver his State of the Union message. In a short speech, President Wilson said he wished to prove for himself that the President of the United States is a person and not a mere department of the government. He also called for new tariff legislation aimed at stimulating foreign trade. This point received loud applause.

Hundreds of people were on hand to witness this historic occasion. All presidents after John Adams had sent written reports to Congress on the state of the union.

L.A. GETS OWENS RIVER WATER

Nov. 5, Los Angeles   Chief City Engineer William Mulholland officially declared the Owens River Aqueduct open today. An amazing engineering feat, the aqueduct will bring 260 million gallons of water a day to this semi-desert city. The water travels 234 miles across extremely rugged terrain, through ditches and pipes, by the natural force of gravity alone.

CROWD HONORS FIVE BRAVE MEN

Feb. 14, London   Today a memorial service was held at St. Paul's Cathedral for Captain Robert Falcon Scott and his companions who died in the Antarctic. Last week a search party found their bodies. They were in a snow-covered tent 10 miles (17 km) from their supply base. Captain Scott's diary tells us what happened. When they reached the South Pole they saw the Norwegian flag flying there. Roald Amundsen's expedition had got there first. They were bitterly disappointed. On the way back the party encountered blinding snowstorms. They had very little food or fuel. They were too weak to reach their supplies.

Captain Scott and his team at the South Pole.

PALATIAL RAIL TERMINAL OPENS

Feb. 2, New York   About 150,000 people came, mainly from the Bronx, Brooklyn, and Manhattan, for the opening of the magnificent new Grand Central Terminal. The ceiling in the main part of the station is decorated with a representation of the night sky, and people craned their necks to admire it. However, many visitors were confused by the building. One attendant said he answered over 300 questions, including queries about where and when trains departed or arrived. Other people were curious about the kind of marble used in the building's construction, the type of architecture, and the complicated electrical system.

DRIVE ENDS IN TRAGEDY

April 20, Paris Today two children with their governess were drowned in a tragic accident. Their car broke down on a hill. When the driver got out, it rolled back down the hill. It crossed a street and fell into a river. The children were a girl of seven and a boy of five. Their mother, Isadora Duncan, is a famous dancer.

PEACE PRIZE TO ELIHU ROOT

Dec. 10, Washington Because one was not formally awarded in 1912, two Nobel Peace Prizes were presented this year. One went to Senator Root of New York. The Nobel Prize Committee commended his tireless efforts on behalf of international peace and his beneficial influence on the recent dispute between the U.S. and Japan.

NEWS IN BRIEF . . .

STRAVINSKY'S BALLET IS HISSED

May 29, Paris Dancers performing Stravinsky's *Le Sacre du Printemps* for the first time could hardly hear the music. A large section of the audience booed and hissed it all the way through. They did not like Stravinsky's unusual music or Nijinsky's sensual dancing. The evening at the ballet ended in uproar.

FULL-LENGTH MOVIES ARE RELEASED

July 12, New York The French movie *Queen Elizabeth* has had its first showing in this country. It stars the famous stage actress Sarah Bernhardt. Earlier in the year a thrilling chariot race was seen in the Italian movie *Quo Vadis?* Long movies like these are now being shown in special theaters.

PANAMA CANAL COMPLETED

Oct. 10, Washington President Wilson pushed a button today, igniting dynamite that blasted open the last of the Panama Canal. Large ships will soon be moving quickly and easily between the Atlantic and Pacific oceans.

DOWN WITH THE NUDE

March 30, Chicago As part of the traveling New York Armory Show, Marcel Duchamp's painting *Nude Descending a Staircase* is now shocking this city. One critic calls it ''an explosion in a pebble factory.''

SCRAPING THE SKY

April 24, New York The new Woolworth Building was lit from top to bottom tonight. At 1,393 feet high, with 55 floors, this is now the tallest building in the entire world.

LADIES' FASHIONS SHOCK AMERICA

Spring, New York Ladies of the smart set are shocking America by wearing Persian trousers. They complete the outfit with embroidered tunics and turbans. On their feet they wear oriental slippers. This strange fashion began when the French government allowed a certain lady archaeologist to wear trousers for her work in Persia. Nobody expected American ladies to copy her and start a new fashion.

AIR JOURNEY ENDS IN DISASTER

Oct. 17, Berlin The world's largest airship, the zeppelin *L2*, has exploded in the worst zeppelin disaster to date. Twenty-seven passengers died. The *L2* flew for the first time only a month ago. Germany's kaiser once called its inventor, Count Zeppelin, ''the greatest man of the century.''

1914

MARCHING TO WAR
HEIR TO AUSTRIA IS SHOT

June 28, Sarajevo The Austrian archduke Franz Ferdinand and his wife, the duchess Sophie, have been shot dead. They were visiting the Bosnian town of Sarajevo. Bosnia, in the Balkans, is part of the Austrian Empire. This is seen as the latest attempt to free the Balkan countries from foreign rule. But the killer was a Serbian, not a Bosnian. His name was Gavrilo Princip.

Franz Ferdinand, archduke of Austria, and the duchess Sophie shortly before the assassination.

SERBIA BLAMED FOR MURDER

Aug. 4, Washington Princip has accidentally started a great war. Austria blamed the Serbians for the archduke's murder, and has declared war on Serbia. Germany has sided with Austria. Three days ago Austria declared war on Russia, which is defending Serbia. France is supporting Russia. German troops are marching toward Paris through Belgium. Britain has a treaty with Belgium and today declared war on Germany.

The Allies	The Central Powers
Russia	Germany
France	Austria
Britain	Turkey
Belgium	
Serbia	

Recruiting offices are being set up all over England. This one is in Trafalgar Square, London. The poster reads "Go! It's your duty, lad."

TROOPS ON A WESTERN FRONT

Aug. 17, Southampton, England Crowds lined the streets today to watch the British Expeditionary Force (BEF) leave for France. They will march to Mons in Belgium, to stop the Germans reaching Paris. The English people are certain the war will be won by Christmas.

GERMANS SCORN BRITISH ARMY

Aug. 23, Belgian Front From a German report: Today we attacked British troops at Mons. They will not stop us reaching Paris. We have many more soldiers than they do. Our Kaiser has called the BEF "a contemptible little army." He assures us of victory before autumn.

BOTH ARMIES MARCH SOUTH

Sept. 2, France After fierce fighting at Mons, the BEF has withdrawn to the south. New boots, and the rough cobbled streets, caused many blistered and swollen feet. The men had very little rest or food. They marched 200 miles (320 km) in 13 days. The Royal Flying Corps is watching from the air as the Germans continue to march toward Paris.

THE WAR CHANGES DIRECTION

Oct. 14, Ypres, Belgium Many of the German soldiers have been recalled to defend their eastern boundary. The Russians are marching toward it. The remaining German troops have been driven back across the Marne River, with heavy casualties. The Allied armies have now marched north to Ypres in Flanders. They are digging trenches for protection on the flat plain. The Germans cannot take Paris, but are trying to get to Calais. Whoever holds the coast will have a great advantage.

NO WINNERS IN TRENCHES

Nov. 11, Ypres After nearly two months of fighting, both sides are exhausted. This trench warfare is quite new. One side shells the other's trenches; then their soldiers advance with rifles and fixed bayonets. The survivors fire on the advancing soldiers. Both sides use these tactics. The shells and the rifle fire cause enormous casualties. British soldiers killed and wounded in three months amount to over 80,000; French casualties are 50,000. In England, over one million men between the ages of 18 and 30 have volunteered for the army. Women are being recruited as nurses.

GERMANY COUNTS ITS LOSSES

Nov. 15, Ypres From a German report: It has begun to snow, and we are preparing for a cold and uncomfortable winter. We have 134,000 dead and wounded. Most of them were very young men, straight from school and university. The survivors are calling this "the massacre of the innocents."

BRITISH WIN FALKLANDS BATTLE

Dec. 11, London The Royal Navy is celebrating today. Four German battleships have been sunk as they tried to capture the Falkland Islands. The British have coal supplies and a radio station at Port Stanley. The Germans did not know that there were two British battleships in the harbor. The battleships came out with guns blazing. Other Royal Navy ships are chasing the rest of the German fleet.

German and British soldiers meet on friendly terms on Christmas Day. British commanders have forbidden this fraternization to happen again.

CHRISTMAS IN THE TRENCHES

Dec. 25, Ypres Over 2 million small brass boxes have arrived from England. They are Christmas presents for the troops and nurses. They contain tobacco or chocolate. This has been a day of goodwill: no guns were fired. Men of both sides walked into no-man's-land. They talked and smoked together. Tomorrow, the fighting will continue.

THE EASTERN FRONT

GERMANS WIN A VICTORY OVER RUSSIA

Aug. 30, Tannenburg, East Prussia General Samsonov has failed to invade Germany. The Russian general hoped to draw German troops away from France. The German 5th Army was badly outnumbered, but their troops are better trained. The Russian Army contains many raw young recruits. The Battle of Tannenburg lasted just four days. The Germans, led by General von Hindenburg, took 120,000 prisoners. General Samsonov shot himself after the battle.

RUSSIANS BATTLE FOR POLAND

Nov. 25, Poland The Russians are fighting to keep the German Army out of Poland. Four days ago they had the Germans surrounded. Suddenly the Germans cut through the Russian lines, taking 16,000 Russian prisoners. The war in the east is slowing down with sub-zero temperatures.

UNIONS GET RIGHT TO STRIKE

April 21, Washington With the new Clayton Antitrust Act, Congress gives organized labor the right to picket and strike. Unions now cannot be prosecuted for these activities.

NEWS IN BRIEF . . .

RAGTIME HIT

July 10, New Orleans Ragtime music, popular since the turn of the century, has produced another hit. This year everyone is singing Harry Carroll's "By the Beautiful Sea." Chorus boys dressed in sailor suits have been helping to sell the sheet music for this song across the country.

DAMSEL ALWAYS IN DISTRESS

April 4, Hollywood Movie-goers love car chases, the rescue of ladies tied to railroad tracks, and similar dramas. An exciting new movie series stars Pearl White, who trained in a circus. She does all the stunts herself. Her adventures will include aeroplane accidents, train wrecks, and fires at sea. Each film will end with Pearl in danger. Movie-goers will have to wait for the next thrilling installment to see if she survives.

20,000 HOMELESS IN JAPAN

Sept. 30, South Kyushu A volcano, Mount Sakurajima, has erupted in Kagoshima Bay. A huge cloud of lava and dust rose 5.5 miles (9 km) into the air. The lava flow joined the mainland to a small island. Seven villages were totally destroyed.

CARS ARE BIG BUSINESS

Jan. 5, Detroit Mr. Ford's car factory was overwhelmed today. Police had to control hundreds of men applying for jobs. The reason for their eagerness is that Mr. Ford is doubling his workers' wages to a minimum of $5 a day. His business, and his wealth, have grown enormously.

Mr. Ford's cars are no longer built one by one. The parts are put together on an assembly line.

1915

THE GALLIPOLI CAMPAIGN
DARDANELLES CLOSED TO SHIPPING

Jan. 1, London The Russians have always reached the Aegean Sea and the Mediterranean through the narrow channel called the Dardanelles (see map). Now the Turks are not allowing any ships through. They are defending the Dardanelles with German Krupp guns. Russia is cut off from her Allies.

ALLIES ATTEMPT DARDANELLES BREAKTHROUGH

March 19, Paris The Allies are trying to send ammunition to Russia to fend off attacks from Turkey. Yesterday a fleet of Allied battleships tried to sail through the Dardanelles. It was a complete disaster: the Turks fired on the fleet from both sides of the peninsula. A French battleship exploded, and two British battleships hit mines and sank. The surviving ships sailed back into the Aegean Sea. Russia is still cut off.

SOLDIERS FACE GAS HORROR

April 22, Ypres In France the Germans are using a new weapon—chlorine gas. It rolled towards Allied lines today in a thick yellowish cloud. It burns the eyes, throat, and lungs. Stretcher bearers are carrying victims to the Red Cross tents behind the lines. German troops advanced today wearing masks over their faces.

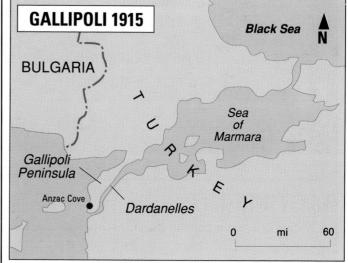

GALLIPOLI 1915

Black Sea

BULGARIA

TURKEY

Sea of Marmara

Gallipoli Peninsula

Anzac Cove

Dardanelles

0   mi   60

ALLIES LAND AT GALLIPOLI

April 25, Cairo Under Turkish fire, the Allies have landed men on the Gallipoli Peninsula, at the entrance to the Dardanelles. The Turks were waiting in ambush as Allied troops landed on the beaches. Hundreds of men were killed. Hospital ships have taken the wounded to Egypt.

The country is rocky and bare. The survivors climbed great cliffs under fire, and then dug trenches for cover. There are too few men left to carry out an effective attack. They are of all nationalities. The British, French, and Sikh troops have been under fire before. New to the war are the Anzacs (Australian and New Zealand Army Corps). However, these troops played a very important part in the landing on the west shore of the Dardanelles.

The Landing by George Lambert shows Anzac troops arriving at the Dardanelles.

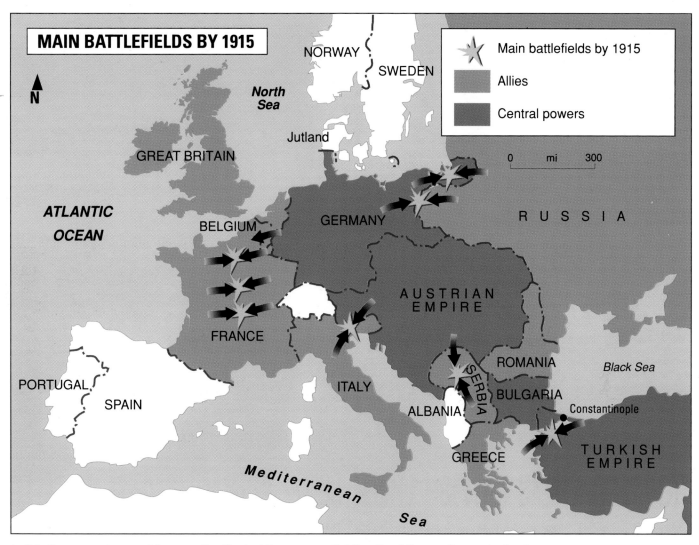

MAIN BATTLEFIELDS BY 1915

N

NORWAY

SWEDEN

North Sea

Jutland

GREAT BRITAIN

ATLANTIC OCEAN

BELGIUM

GERMANY

RUSSIA

AUSTRIAN EMPIRE

ROMANIA

Black Sea

FRANCE

PORTUGAL

SPAIN

ITALY

SERBIA

BULGARIA

Constantinople

ALBANIA

GREECE

TURKISH EMPIRE

Mediterranean Sea

Main battlefields by 1915

Allies

Central powers

0   mi   300

In this the second year of the war, the Central Powers are fighting the Allies on five major fronts.

French soldiers in their trenches.

Turkish guns at Gallipoli.

British troop positions at Anzac Cove.

TORPEDO SINKS BRITISH LINER

May 8, Washington The largest passenger ship in the world, the *Lusitania*, has been torpedoed by a German submarine, or U-boat. U-boats have sunk hundreds of merchant ships. The Germans are trying to stop food reaching Britain. But this attack on an unarmed ship has shocked everyone. Over 100 Americans were among the 1,200 people drowned. President Wilson is going to protest to Germany. People are wondering how long he can keep the United States out of the war.

SOME GERMAN PLANS REVEALED

July 24, New York Although the United States and Germany are not at war, German secret agents are spying in America. A U.S. secret service man followed a suspect, and snatched his briefcase. It contained plans to wreck American ships and factories. The Germans had also arranged for American theaters to show pro-German movies, and for American newspapers to carry pro-German articles. Two German officials have been told to leave the U.S.

NO ADVANCE AT GALLIPOLI

June 25, London The Allies have landed more troops at Gallipoli. It is intensely hot, water is short, and many men have died of dysentery. The fighting goes on day and night. The Anzacs are particularly daring, but every time they attack, fierce Turkish fire holds them back. The Turkish force, led by Mustafa Kemal, is small but courageous. The Turks are determined not to surrender the peninsula. If they did, the Allies could take the Turkish capital.

TROOPS LEAVE GALLIPOLI

Dec. 31, London The Germans are sending troops to help the Turks. The Allies cannot hope to win now. By night, and in bitterly cold weather, Allied soldiers are quietly boarding troop ships. They are leaving their supplies behind. The retreat will go on into the New Year. The campaign has left 30,000 dead and 74,000 wounded. Nothing has been won, only the fame of valiant men. The Anzacs' bravery will never be forgotten.

NURSE SHOT IN BELGIUM

Oct. 12, Brussels Miss Edith Cavell, a British nurse, was shot by the Germans this morning. She ran the Brussels School of Nursing. She nursed any wounded soldier, whatever his nationality. The Germans discovered that she also helped British soldiers to escape. They executed her for treason.

SERBIA IS DEFEATED

Dec. 21, Serbia The Germans now occupy the whole of Poland. The Bulgarians have joined with the Germans and captured Serbia. Hundreds of starving Serbians are escaping to Albania.

Nurse Edith Cavell at home.

NEWS IN BRIEF . . .

MOVIE THREATENS RACE TENSION

Feb. 8, Los Angeles An epic film, *The Birth of a Nation*, is seen as America's answer to the successful Italian film *Quo Vadis?* But some Negro leaders have protested. The film shows the early history of the violent Ku Klux Klan. They are afraid it may lead to a Klan revival.

INDIAN LAWYER SIDES WITH POOR

Nov. 22, Bombay An Indian lawyer, Mr. Mohandas Gandhi, has returned home from South Africa. During his 20 years in South Africa he encouraged Africans to resist unjust laws, but without violence. Mr. Gandhi led demonstrations, and wrote newspaper articles. He went to prison for his beliefs. The prime minister of South Africa, General Jan Smuts, respected his ideals. Mr. Gandhi has become a hero to Indian nationalists.

CHICAGO BEGINS DRY SUNDAYS

Oct. 10, Chicago The mayor of Chicago has outlawed the sale of alcoholic beverages on Sundays. Ministers and reformers are delighted with the new law, the first of its kind in 43 years. Chicago's police chief reported only a few violations of the new measure so far.

TELEPHONE CALL ACROSS THE ATLANTIC

Oct. 21, Washington In January, Alexander Bell, inventor of the telephone, phoned right across the American continent. Today a message was sent from the eastern United States across the Atlantic Ocean to Paris.

FASHION NEWS

Spring, Paris Ladies' hats are smaller this year. They have broad, deep crowns and wide brims. Skirts are worn just above the ankle, to show leather shoes or ankle boots with 2 inch (5 cm) heels. Men's shoes are often covered with cloth spats.

A POET DIES AT SEA

April 23, Greece Mr. Rupert Brooke, the poet, died today of blood poisoning. He was 27. He was an officer on a ship sailing for the Dardanelles. His most famous poem "The Soldier" begins:

If I should die, think only this of me:
That there's some corner of a foreign field
That is for ever England . . .

That "corner" will be on the Greek island of Skyros.

GREAT EXPLORER IS RESCUED

Aug. 30, London Two years ago Mr. Ernest Shackleton set out with a team of explorers to cross Antarctica. His ship, *Endurance,* was caught in pack ice on the Weddell Sea in January 1915. For nine months it drifted helplessly. At last the party managed to reach a deserted island. In order to get help for his exhausted men, Mr. Shackleton sailed alone in a small open boat for 780 miles (1,300 km) to South Georgia Island, which he crossed on foot. He reached a whaling station that had a wireless transmitter. A relief expedition has now picked up all the men.

Ernest Shackleton in arctic gear.

"HOLY" RASPUTIN IS DEAD

Dec. 30, St. Petersburg Two Russian noblemen have murdered the extraordinary Gregori Rasputin. Ten years ago this man treated the only son of the tsar and tsarina of Russia, who has hemophilia. Rasputin became the adviser of the tsarina, and through her, of the tsar himself. But he was not the holy man the tsarina thought him. Russians believed his influence was evil. Rasputin survived poison, so his murderers shot him. Still alive, he was thrown into a river where he drowned.

WILSON REELECTED

Nov. 7, Washington Woodrow Wilson has been reelected President of the United States. One of the reasons for his popularity is that many Americans feel he is responsible for keeping us out of the conflict in Europe. In fact, a major Democratic campaign slogan was "He kept us out of the war." It now remains to be seen how long he will be able to continue doing so.

Four world leaders. Woodrow Wilson is on the right.

A VIEW FROM THE TRENCHES

France "If only the people of England could have seen what I saw yesterday they would not grumble about air raids. I saw motor lorries sunk in the mud over the wheels, also horses with just part of their heads showing above the swamp, also 2 tanks which were in the Push and were buried — the men who were still in them will never be able to tell the tale of the fight but they were heroes.

. . . There are men now in the trenches full of water who are nearly dead, they are fast dying of cold, they go sick, see the doctor, go back and try to stick it until they get relieved . . ."

(Daniel Sweeney, a soldier, from *Greater Love,* ed. M. Moynihan, W.H. Allen 1980)

UNITED STATES TROOPS ENTER MEXICO

June 21, Mexico United States troops have crossed the border into Mexico. They are searching for a rebel named Pancho Villa. He has led raids across the Mexican border into North America. In January his soldiers stripped and shot 18 American miners. Similar incidents followed. Americans are taking tough action to protect United States citizens. There is fear that a full-scale war may break out between the two countries.

The outlaw Pancho Villa and his men.

NEWS IN BRIEF . . .

SANGER FAVORS BIRTH CONTROL

Oct. 16, New York Margaret Sanger says poverty cannot be overcome until people limit family size. Mrs. Sanger, a public health nurse, has given much of her time to the care of poor women in this city.

SERBS SALUTE EXTRAORDINARY WOMAN

Nov. 30, Belgrade Flora Sandes was nursing in Serbia when the army fled into Albania last December. She dressed as a man and joined the army. She was seriously wounded fighting the Turks. The grateful Serbs have given her a medal for bravery.

JEANNETTE RANKIN FIRST WOMAN ELECTED TO CONGRESS

Nov. 7, Washington Jeannette Rankin of Montana, beat her Democratic opponent to become the first woman to be elected to the Congress of the United States. Miss Rankin campaigned by riding back and forth across the state on horseback, talking to as many people as possible. She is a persuasive speaker. An active suffragist, Miss Rankin had many female supporters.

MOVIES MAKE MONEY

Oct. 31, Hollywood Six years ago Hollywood was a small, quiet country town surrounded by lemon groves. Now 52 movie companies have their head-quarters here. The movie business has become the fifth largest American industry. Charlie Chaplin earns more than does the President of the United States. "America's sweetheart," Mary Pickford, earns a million dollars a year.

Film star Mary Pickford.

1917

REVOLUTION IN RUSSIA

MORALE LOW FOR ARMY AND CIVILIANS

January, Petrograd The tsars of Russia rule over a huge country where life is harsh for most people. Rich noble families live in splendid houses while those who work for them live in dreadful poverty. To add to their discontent, the Russian people are sick of the war. They have asked the government to make peace with Germany. The army is short of ammunition and warm clothing. Soldiers are deserting from the Russian front. Tsar Nicholas II is in charge of the army. People blame him for the deaths of two million men in battle.

TSAR DEPOSED BY GENERALS

March 15, Petrograd The army generals told the tsar that he must give up his throne. He has done nothing about the food shortages and general unrest. Starving people are rioting all over the country. Factory workers are on strike. The railroad system has broken down. The temperature is below zero, and there is little firewood or coal.

BOLSHEVIKS SEIZE THEIR CHANCE

April 20, Petrograd Vladimir Lenin, leader of the Bolshevik (socialist) party, wants to replace the weak government. He has called for an end to the unpopular war; and he wants to nationalize the country's industry.

RED REVOLUTION SUCCEEDS

Nov. 7, Petrograd Lenin's Red Guards seized the Winter Palace today. This is where the government has its offices. The Guards locked the government ministers in the palace cellars. Lenin is ready to form his own government. He has achieved the first of his aims.

LENIN'S REFORMS BEGIN

Dec. 5, Brest-Litovsk The new Bolshevik government has signed an armistice with Germany. For the Russians, the war is over. Lenin wants factories to be controlled by workers' councils (soviets). The government will take over farms belonging to the Church, to landlords, and to rich farmers. Lenin's slogan is "Peace, freedom, and bread."

A portrait of Lenin, the Bolshevik leader.

NEWS FROM THE WAR ZONES

ALLIES FACE HINDENBURG LINE

March 30, Flanders From a German report: Our armies have been digging fortified trenches behind the front line, from Arras to Soissons. This Hindenburg Line is about 31 miles (50 km) long. It has concrete dugouts, and is served by railroads which bring in supplies. In front are many fences of barbed wire. No Allied troops will be able to cross it.

AMERICA DECLARES WAR

April 6, Washington Congress has declared war on the Germans. In a speech to Congress on April 2, the President said "The world must be made safe for democracy." The Allies are overjoyed at the news of America's entry.

MUD AND RAIN ADD TO MISERY

August 30, France Today, near the village of Passchendaele, one of the worst battles of the war is being fought. It rains all the time. Soldiers fight ankle-deep in thick mud. Mules and wounded men drown in shell-holes. The hail of bullets and shells never stops. Nobody who survives this battle will ever forget Passchendaele.

MILLIONS JOINING THE ARMY

June 5, Washington Recruiting offices were open for 12 hours today. The response was incredible. Nearly 10 million men have joined the U.S. Army. Recruiting posters all over the country show Uncle Sam saying "I want YOU for the U.S. Army." The new theme song is "Over There" — "there" being the Western Front.

Recruiting posters like this one encourage Americans to join the war effort.

ITALIANS FLEE AUSTRIAN ADVANCE

Nov. 9, northeast Italy The Italians joined the Allies two years ago. They have been fighting the Austrians with some success. But today they were defeated at Caporetto. They have lost a huge area to the German and Austrian armies. Thousands were killed. Italian survivors had to leave their weapons behind as they retreated. Peace in Europe seems to be as far away as ever.

1917

PLANES BOMB LONDON

June 14, London German planes made a daylight bombing raid yesterday. A bomb fell on a school, killing many children. Another hit a train. In the past, zeppelins have been used as bombers. Planes are faster, and not so easy to hit as the airships.

JEWS DELIGHTED BY BALFOUR'S DECLARATION

Nov. 8, Palestine Mr. Arthur Balfour, the British foreign secretary, has declared support for a Jewish national home in Palestine. The Jews are scattered all over the world. Many hope they will have their own homeland at last.

ENGLAND FACES FOOD SHORTAGES

March 20, London There is only about a month's supply of wheat in England. There is a shortage of other foods as well. The shortages are caused by the U-boats, German torpedo-carrying submarines, which sink a quarter of all the ships coming into British ports. This month the Germans have sunk 134 neutral ships as well.

WOMEN URGED TO JOIN FORCES

Nov. 29, London The British Admiralty is going to recruit women into the navy. They will be called the Women's Royal Naval Service (WRNS). Members of the Women's Army Auxiliary Corps (WAAC) are already in France. They work just behind the front lines, in the kitchens, the store rooms, and the offices.

NEWS IN BRIEF . . .

RED CROSS IS HONORED

Dec. 10, Stockholm The International Red Cross has won this year's Nobel Peace Prize. Red Cross volunteers are working in appalling conditions on the battlefronts. Thousands of soldiers owe their lives to the gallant Red Cross.

OLD CONTEMPTIBLES REMEMBERED

Aug. 25, London A new medal, the Mons Star, will be given to those who fought at Mons and Ypres. They will be known as the "Old Contemptibles." (The kaiser called them "a contemptible little army.")

Another medal was awarded for the first time today. It is for civilians who have served Britain and the empire well. The medal is called the Order of the British Empire (OBE).

END OF A LEGEND

Jan. 10, Denver Buffalo Bill, whose real name was William Cody, died today. As a young man he was an army scout during wars against the Indians in the "Wild West." Many legends grew up about his courage and daring, and the thousands of buffaloes he had shot. In 1883 he started a Wild West Show, which toured the country. One of his star performers was a young woman called Annie Oakley, who was a crack shot. She once shot the ash off a cigarette in the mouth of the kaiser! The Wild West Show lasted for 30 years. Everyone wanted to see Buffalo Bill.

FROM TSAR TO STAR?

March, Hollywood Mr. Lewis J. Selznick, the movie producer, has invited ex-Tsar Nicholas to act in movies. Mr. Selznick is an immigrant from Russia. The ex-tsar is not likely to accept this strange invitation.

JUDGE SAYS NO TO BIRTH CONTROL

Sept. 30, New York Miss Margaret Sanger has been sentenced to jail. She opened a birth control clinic last year. The judge said birth control was against the law of the state, and the law of God.

Margaret Sanger, pioneer of birth control.

1918

GERMANS PUSH THE ALLIES BACK

April 10, Marne River, France The year has started badly for the Allies. A week ago, a million German soldiers left the Hindenburg Line and advanced toward the Marne River. They bombarded Allied trenches for five hours, with 6,000 guns and with gas shells. Their new super-gun, nicknamed "Big Bertha," fired on Paris from 62 miles (100 km) away. These guns can fire shells a distance of 75 miles (120 km). For 16 days the whole Allied army had to retreat as the Germans pressed forward.

A new German offensive started yesterday along the Lys River in Belgium. However, it appears that in that area the Allies are holding fast. Both Allied and German losses are heavy.

One of the huge long-range guns in action on the Western Front.

GERMANS LOSE ACE PILOT

April 21, France Everybody on the Somme has heard of the "Red Baron." This German airman flew in his red plane with great skill and daring. Now he has been shot down and killed. Allied soldiers took souvenirs from the plane, and formed a guard of honor at his funeral. Although thousands of airmen on both sides have been killed in this war, they felt that the Red Baron was special.

Baron Manfred von Richthofen — the "Red Baron."

ALLIES SUDDENLY GAIN GROUND

Aug. 8, Amiens The big offensive in April exhausted German troops. Away from the Hindenburg Line they are not so well protected; they are short of food and medical supplies. The Allies have sent in 450 tanks to batter the German gun positions, and their planes are bombing the trenches. Thousands of American soldiers are arriving each month in good health and eager to fight. Hundreds of Germans are surrendering every day.

The French and British advance near Amiens.

TURKS ARE OUT OF WAR

Oct. 3, Damascus British troops under General Edmund Allenby have been fighting the Turks in Judaea and Palestine. They have now captured Damascus. Arab troops from the Hejaz have turned the Turks out of Arabia. They have also arrived at Damascus. The Arabs are led by Emir Feisal, son of the sherif of Mecca, and an Englishman, Lt. Col. T.E. Lawrence. The Turks offered a large reward for Lawrence, dead or alive. He led attacks on many Turkish troop trains. Turkey is now finally defeated.

"T. E. Lawrence," painted by James McBey

RUSSIAN ROYAL FAMILY MURDERED

July 16, Siberia The ex-tsar of Russia, his wife, three daughters, and young son were shot dead today. They have been under house arrest in this remote part of the country. Their killers were the powerful Bolshevik security police, the Cheka.

Tsar Nicholas II of Russia with his son Alexis.

WILSON'S 14 POINTS FOR PEACE

Jan. 8, Washington Before a joint session of Congress, President Wilson set forth his ideas for achieving a peaceful postwar world. He named 14 points to serve as guidelines. Included were open covenants of peace, with no secret agreements; freedom of the seas; equality in trade among nations; and reduction of armaments. Wilson's last point was the formation of an association of nations to safeguard independence and territorial integrity for all countries.

AN ARMISTICE IS SIGNED AT LAST

Nov. 11, Forest of Compiègne, France Four years of continuous fighting ended at 11 A.M. today. In France and Belgium, the two sides have fought over the same territory all this time. Now the guns are at last silent. Turkey and Austria are already out of the war. The German kaiser has fled to Holland, and Germany has been declared a republic. Much of France and Belgium is in ruins.

Allied and German leaders sign the armistice agreement in a railroad car.

One of the tasks facing Europe after the war is to erect lasting tributes to the fallen soldiers. These rows of war graves are at Arras in France.

MORE WOMEN IN FACTORIES

Aug. 1, Chicago There are now a million women working in factories throughout the United States. Many are taking the place of men who have joined the armed forces. However, most female factory employees are not working in any kind of heavy industry. Many labor unions will not accept women or help them obtain fair treatment. In some areas, over 90 percent of women workers are paid less for doing the same work as men. There is the expectation that women will leave these jobs when the men return from war. This is seen as their patriotic duty by some employers.

FLU KILLING MILLIONS WORLDWIDE

Oct. 31, Washington Public health officials here and abroad estimate that the influenza epidemic now sweeping the world may cause as many as 20 million deaths. The U.S. Bureau of Public Health reports that hundreds of thousands of Americans have already died of this disease.

The new flu germ seems to have appeared in Spain first. From Europe it spread to America and Asia. It is believed that millions have died in China alone. Attempts to find a cure have failed.

AMERICA GAINS WHILE EUROPE DECLINES

Dec., New York America has come out of the war without the ruin that faces other countries. Business has boomed, and factories have been working around the clock. The U.S.A. is now in a very favorable position, and may very well become the leading nation of the world.

POET WHO DENIED THAT WAR IS "GLORIOUS"

Nov. 4, France The noted poet Wilfred Owen has been killed in action. Many hundreds of young men were taught at home and at school that death in battle was valiant and noble. They learned a Latin phrase which means "It is sweet and fitting to die for one's country." In one poem, Owen called this "the old lie." His poetry reflects war's stupidity and waste.

NEWS IN BRIEF . . .

MUSIC JOINED THE WAR EFFORT

Nov. 30, New York While America was at war, the city's orchestra refused to play music by living German composers. Many Americans extended this ban to all German composers. They refused to listen to music by Beethoven, Brahms, or Mozart.

KINDERGARTENS TO OPEN

Aug. 17, Washington The U.S. Bureau of Education announced that its general guidelines for opening kindergartens have been adopted by five states: Maine, Oregon, Tennessee, Texas, and Washington. The Congress of Mothers and other groups have been working for the establishment of kindergartens across the nation. The number of these classes is growing rapidly.

AIR ACE DOWNS 26th GERMAN

Oct. 20, Paris Captain Eddie Rickenbacker of the American Army Air Service has scored 14 victories over the enemy this month. That raised his total destruction score to 22 aircraft and four observation balloons. Rickenbacker began his flying career relatively late, at the age of 26, a year before he joined the Army. But he has been making up for lost time ever since.

1919

PEACE PROPOSALS IN PARIS

PRESIDENT SUGGESTS LEAGUE OF WORLD NATIONS

Feb. 14, Paris In the Palace of Versailles, delegates from 51 nations are working out a peace treaty. All these nations want to avoid war in the future. It is difficult to decide how this can be done. President Woodrow Wilson has suggested that they should form a council called the "League of Nations." He would like America to belong to it.

GERMANS MUST PAY FOR THE WAR

May 7, Paris The peace treaty has finally been agreed on, after much discussion. President Wilson wanted Europeans to forget the war and start afresh. The French, who have to rebuild their towns and villages, want Germany to pay heavily. The treaty they have drawn up says that Germany started the war, and must pay "reparations" of about $33 billion to the Allies, and must reduce its army and weapons. The conference agreed that a League of Nations should be set up.

GERMANS DISAGREE WITH PEACE PROPOSALS

May 31, Paris The German chancellor has resigned rather than sign the peace treaty. The Germans say they took no part in drawing it up. They do not agree that they were the only country responsible for the war. They are also shocked at the size of the reparations. But the Allies will not back down.

POLAND HAS A CORRIDOR TO DANZIG

June 28, Warsaw Poland has been part of Russia for 50 years. A clause in the peace treaty has made it an independent country. It has been given a strip of land crossing German territory. This will give it an outlet to the Baltic Sea. It will be able to use the port of Danzig. Danzig, once German, has been made a "free city" by the Treaty of Versailles.

GERMAN FLEET SUNK

June 21, Scapa Flow, Scotland German prisoners-of-war sank seventy of their own ships in Scapa Flow harbor today. The Allies are shocked at this action. The ships were docked at this remote port while the Paris Peace Conference decided what to do with them. The German admiral says he was obeying an order never to surrender his warships.

German sailors arrive on shore after scuttling their ship at Scapa Flow.

PEACE TREATY SIGNED IN SILENCE

June 28, Paris This afternoon two German representatives came to the Palace of Versailles. They entered the Hall of Mirrors, where the president of the United States, the prime minister of Great Britain, and the premiers of France and Italy sat in silence. The Germans signed the Versailles Peace Treaty. Without speaking, they walked out of the hall. The German nation feels it has been forced into accepting terms that are unreasonable.

The silent German delegation at Versailles.

GERMAN UNREST LEADS TO UPRISING

Jan. 15, Berlin The murder in custody of Rosa Luxembourg and Karl Liebnecht has shocked Germany. They were leaders of a Communist group called the "Sparticists." In Germany's confused state, political parties with violent aims are being formed. The Sparticists tried to start a revolution. Another new group, the Frei Korps, is being blamed for the murders. Though they helped the government troops defeat the Sparticists, they also threaten Germany's future.

INNOCENT BYSTANDERS MASSACRED AT AMRITSAR

April 13, Amritsar, India Thousands of people were gathered today in a public walled garden in the city. Many were in Amritsar as pilgrims to the holy Sikh temple. Others had gone to listen to Indian speakers protest about new British government laws. Last week public meetings were banned because of serious rioting in Amritsar. General Dyer, who commands British and Indian troops, heard about the gathering. He marched 50 Gurkha soldiers into the garden and ordered them to fire on the crowd. They fired for 10 minutes. Most of the Indians were killed; many were young children. This brutal attack will make Indians more determined to break away from the British Empire.

ANTI-GOVERNMENT PROTEST IN CHINA

Nov. 4, Peking, China By the peace settlement, Japan was given a part of the Chinese province of Shantung, which was once German territory. The Chinese government accepted this decision. But on May 4, three thousand students from the new Peking University demonstrated against it in Tian-an-men Square. The demonstration was peaceful until someone attacked a pro-Japanese official. Then government troops arrested over 1,000 young men and women. Students in 200 towns also demonstrated against the government. The public supported the students: shops closed, and factories went on strike. The government has been forced to release the jailed students.

In March, Marconi used this wireless telephone to transmit signals from Ireland to Nova Scotia.

HERO HOLDS PORT

Sept. 23, Italy Signor Gabriele D'Annunzio, with 2,000 men, has occupied Fiume. Fiume used to be part of the Austrian Empire, but it has a large Italian population. Earlier this year it became a "free" port under League of Nations protection. Signor D'Annunzio has popular support, but not the approval of the Italian government.

THE FASCISTS ARE A GROWING PARTY

Oct. 31, Milan Benito Mussolini, an Italian journalist, founded a new political party called the Fascists last March. After only seven months it has a membership of 17,000. The Fascists want many reforms. These include more land for the peasants, pensions, and an eight-hour day in factories. The Fascist party appeals to many Italians.

NEWS IN BRIEF . . .

TRIUMPH FOR AMERICAN WOMEN

June 4, Washington The United States Constitution has been amended. In the future, no citizen will be denied the right to vote because of her or his sex. The suffragettes have won their fight for the right to vote.

BOXER'S WIN IS A WALK-OVER

July 4, Toledo, Ohio Jack Dempsey has become the world heavy-weight boxing champion. He defeated Jess Willard so heavily that spectators called for the fight to be stopped. The huge Jess Willard seemed astonished at Dempsey's power. He is unlikely to continue boxing.

STYLISH WIMBLEDON

July 5, Wimbledon, England France's 20-year-old Suzanne Lenglen has beaten the British champion Dorothea Chambers. It was also a meeting of old and new styles of dress. Miss Chambers wore the usual ankle-length dress with long sleeves. By comparison, Miss Lenglen looked freer and cooler in a short-sleeved blouse and calf-length skirt.

PROHIBITION RATIFIED

Jan. 29, Washington An amendment to the Constitution that prohibits the sale of alcoholic beverages has been approved by three-fourths of the states. Acting Secretary of State Polk issued the historic proclamation. It goes into effect January 16, 1920.

A gloomy view of prohibition.

FIVE COUNTRIES HAVE LOST THEIR HEADS

Dec. 30 Since 1910, five countries have decided not to be ruled by a king or emperor. Instead, they will have an elected leader. Portugal, China, Russia, Austria, and Germany were all monarchies or empires ten years ago, and now they are all republics.

RELATIVITY IS RIGHT

March 29, London "The greatest genius on earth" is how Albert Einstein is now described. Members of the Royal Society of London took photographs of a total eclipse of the sun. They made many calculations, based on the photographs. These show that Einstein's Theory of Relativity is correct.

Albert Einstein, the physicist.

PEOPLE OF THE NINETEEN-TENS

David Lloyd George, British politician 1863–1945

Lloyd George entered Parliament as a Liberal in 1890. He was chancellor of the exchequer from 1908 to 1915. He became prime minister in 1916, and was recognized as a great war leader. He resigned in 1922, and held no more public positions. Lloyd George was a charming man, and a witty debater. He came from a poor background, and fought for social reform, introducing health and unemployment benefits in 1911. He sympathized with the Irish desire for freedom, and started the talks that led to the Government of Ireland Act of 1920.

Jan Christiaan Smuts, South African leader 1870–1950

Smuts fought against the British in South Africa in the Boer War of 1899. He was a very daring guerrilla fighter. He became pro-British when the British government granted self-rule to South Africa in 1909. During World War I his forces attacked German colonies in East Africa. In 1917 he became a member of the Allied War Cabinet. He helped to create the RAF. In 1919 he became prime minister of the Union of South Africa. He opposed apartheid but was not able to stop it. Smuts welcomed the League of Nations in 1919, and the United Nations Organization in 1945.

Woodrow Wilson, American politician 1856–1924

Wilson was elected President of the United States in 1912, and he held this position until 1920. He tried to keep America out of World War I. But when the Germans continued to attack American ships, and particularly the civilian *Lusitania*, he finally asked Congress to declare war in 1917, in order to make the world "safe for democracy." He proved to be a great wartime leader. After the war, Wilson was a leading figure at the Peace Conference. The League of Nations was his idea. Although he urged the Senate to join the League, it refused to do so. Wilson fell ill in 1919. He retired from politics a disappointed man.

Vladimir Ilyich Lenin 1870–1924

Lenin was the leader of the Bolsheviks in Russia. He was a well-educated and intelligent man. Lenin became a revolutionary when his brother was hanged in 1887 (he had been in a plot to kill Tsar Alexander). Lenin spent his youth dodging the police, or in exile. He hoped World War I would end capitalism. Then the workers of the world might rule their own countries.

In Russia in 1917, he seized his chance. Over the next five years he became a dictator and crushed other political parties, bringing communism to the whole Russian empire. In his last years he regretted the path Bolshevism was taking. He thought Stalin would be bad for the country.

Sarah Bernhardt, French actress 1844–1923

Sarah Bernhardt's American debut in 1880 was so popular that tickets were being sold on the black market. Audiences loved this tiny actress with the golden voice. She continued to play the role of young women into her 50s with great success. In 1912 she starred in two French movies: *Queen Elizabeth* and *The Lady of the Camellias*. Two years later she had to have a leg amputated, but she continued to act. The French government made her a member of the Legion of Honor.

Erich von Ludendorff, German general 1865–1937

General von Ludendorff was chief of staff to Paul von Hindenburg in World War I. He took part in the first march into Belgium in 1914. He was transferred to the Eastern Front and defeated General Samsonov at the Battle of Tannenburg. His strategy caused the defeat of the Serbians, and the Italians at Caporetto. The Hindenburg Line was his idea. He agreed that the Germans should sink ships of all nations.

In 1917 he helped Lenin return to Russia from Switzerland, putting him on a special sealed train through Germany. He hoped that a Russian revolution would help the German war effort. The following year he planned the last great German offensive. When it failed, he asked the kaiser to make peace. He was dismissed on October 26. For a time in the 1920s and 1930s he backed Hitler. But after a lifetime of war, he became a pacifist.

Isadora Duncan, American dancer 1878–1927

Isadora Duncan based her dancing on the figures painted on Greek vases. She shocked people in many countries because of her see-through clothing and bare feet. Once the Berlin police banned her performance, saying it was obscene.

Americans were scandalized by her private life. She had many lovers, and two illegitimate children. Both children were drowned in an accident in 1913. In 1921 she was invited to Moscow, and Lenin gave her a house to live in. She taught dancing there, and married a Russian poet. He was mentally ill, and in 1925 he hanged himself. Isadora died in a freak accident in France. She was in an open car when her long red scarf caught in the spoked wheel. As the car sped on, the scarf strangled her.

American Firsts

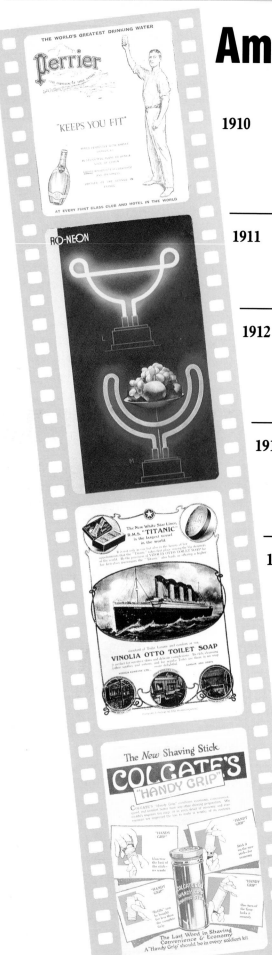

1910   Father's Day first celebrated, Spokane, Wash.
First aircraft takeoff from the deck of a ship, off Hampton Roads, Va.
First American aviation meet held, Los Angeles, Calif.

1911   Electric self-starter for cars demonstrated at General Motors in Michigan.
First annual Indianapolis 500 auto race held in Indianapolis, Ind.

1912   New flying boat demonstrated by Glenn Curtis, San Diego, Calif.
Curative values of vitamins A and B discovered by Elmer McCollum at Yale University in Conn.

1913   First time U.S. senators elected by popular vote instead of by state legislators.
Wireless message by telegraph successfully transmitted across the ocean from Arlington, Va. to Paris, France.

1914   American Society of Composers, Authors, and Publishers (ASCAP) organized in New York City.
Theodore W. Richards was first American to win Nobel Prize in Chemistry.
Mother's Day, celebrated the second Sunday in May, established by Congress.

1915   U.S. Coast Guard established by Congress.
First transcontinental phone call made from New York City to San Francisco, Calif.
Washington Square Players (later the Theater Guild), Neighborhood Playhouse, and Provincetown Players were established.

1916   New York City building code changed to allow skyscrapers of unlimited height.
National Park Service established as part of the Department of the Interior.
First annual Tournament of Roses football game played in Pasadena, Calif.

1917	First Pulitzer Prizes awarded.
	First double no-hit nine-inning baseball game played in Chicago: Chicago Cubs lost to Cincinnati Reds in the tenth inning.
1918	Post Office issued first airmail stamps.
	First airmail service with regular runs between New York City and Washington, D.C. established.
	Typewriting speed record of 170 words per minute made by Margaret Owen.
1919	*The American Language* by H. L. Mencken published.
	Daily airmail service between Chicago and New York City established.
	First municipal airport in the country opened in Tucson, Ariz.

New words and expressions

The English language is always changing. New words are added to it, and old words are used in new ways. Here are a few of the words and expressions that first appeared or first came into popular use in the 1910s:

airplane (for aeroplane)	good egg
allergy	intelligence test
alligator (jazz musician)	It's a cinch
backpack	jazz
have something on the ball	jitney
	joyride
big shot	lowbrow
boner	lunatic fringe
bum steer	money talks
collage	motorcade
cellophane	motorize
camouflage	to be off base
comic strip	pitcher's mound
conk out	pinch hitter
clean up (as in stock market)	radio station
	rattletrap
cutting remark	let slip
dog tag	spill the beans
duck soup	string along

How many of these words and expressions do we still use today? Do you know what they all mean?

Glossary

amendment: a change or addition to a document.

aqueduct: a structure for carrying a large amount of flowing water, usually over long distances.

armistice: agreement to stop a war.

Bolsheviks: members of a Russian political party. They believed in rule by the people, not by a tsar. They were the original Communist party.

campaigned: ran for public office; worked to bring about a specific goal.

concerto: music for a solo instrument, accompanied by an orchestra.

coup: an illegal change of government. Short for *coup d' état,* which means "a blow at the state."

dominion: a self-governing territory of the British Commonwealth.

dynasty: a family of rulers.

Fascists: Italian political party, anti-Communist. Its leader, Benito Mussolini, ruled Italy as a dictator. The name comes from Latin. *Fasces* (bundles of rods) were carried in front of the Roman emperor as a sign of his authority.

free city: a city that rules itself, and does not belong to any one nation.

gunboat: a small armed ship.

influenza: a viral disease. Sufferers have fever and aching limbs.

Ku Klux Klan: a secret racist society of whites formed in the southern states after the Civil War.

lorries: a British term for motortrucks.

monopolies: sole ownership or control of certain products or services.

no-man's-land: territory between opposing sides in a war, claimed by neither.

parole: word of honor. A prisoner on parole is allowed to live at home; he gives his word not to escape.

picket: to stand outside a workplace to persuade people to respect a strike, or to demonstrate or protest.

prohibition: a 1920 law forbidding the sale of alcoholic beverages in the U.S. This law was canceled in 1933.

radium: a radioactive metal.

reparations: compensation for war damage.

Sikh: a member of an Indian religious group.

spats: a short cover for men's shoes. Spats were made of cloth and were fastened under the shoe with a strap.

suffragettes: women who campaigned for the vote (suffrage).

treason: the crime of plotting the overthrow of one's government.

whaling station: a permanent base for the whale hunting process.

Further Reading

Bosco, Peter. *World War I.* Facts on File, 1991

Cairns, Trevor. *Twentieth Century.* Lerner, 1984

Carey, Helen and Greenberg, Judith. *How to Read a Newspaper.* Watts, 1983

——*How to Use Primary Sources.* Watts, 1983

Collins, David R. *Woodrow Wilson: Twenty-Eighth President of the United States.* Garrett Ed., 1989

Humble, Richard. *U-Boat.* Watts, 1990

Jantzen, Steven L. *Hooray for Peace, Hurrah for War: The United States During World War I.* Facts on File, 1990

Maynard, Christopher and Jefferis, David. *The Aces: Pilots and Planes of World War I.* Watts, 1987

Ross, Stewart. *The Origins of World War I.* Watts, 1989

——*War in the Trenches: World War One.* Watts

Smith, Betsy C. *Women Win the Vote.* Silver Burdett Pr., 1989

Sullivan, George. *Famous Blimps and Airships.* Putnam

Index